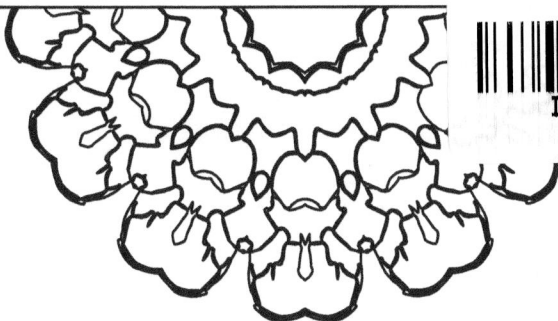

RETURNING

exhortations, advice and encouragement
from the heart of direct realization practice

shambhavi sarasvati

Jaya Kula Press
110 Marginal Way, #196
Portland, Maine 04101
jayakula.org

Cover design: Shambhavi Sarasvati
Interior design and layout: Cecilia Sorochin/ SoroDesign

Sarasvati, Shambhavi
Returning: exhortations, advice and encouragement from
the heart of direct realization practice
ISBN:
978-0-9841634-4-1
0-9841634-4-1
Printed in the United States of America on acid-free paper.

for waking up hearts

ABOUT THIS BOOK

Returning is a small offering written from the heart to the hearts of my students and also as a reminder to myself.

When we are trying to wake up, we encounter many distractions and diversions. Some of these are circumstances, some our own appetites. Mostly we are distracted by our fixed concepts about ourselves and life.

If we want to discover our real nature, we must learn to follow what incites us to act honestly, open-heartedly and fearlessly, rather than listening to the clamoring of fears, distractions and diversions.

Having enjoyed the opportunity to go astray and be corrected by the grace of my teachers innumerable times, I have published this little book based on my own experience. May it be of benefit.

Shambhavi Sarasvati
August 2015
Andover, Maine

HOW TO USE THIS BOOK

Read it. Any order is fine.

Write in it. Don't be shy.

Feed it. With your courage.

Wear it. As your armor.

Move to it. And any other heart music you can find.

1

If you feel longing to discover your real nature, treat it as the greatest gift.

Never set your longing aside. Don't let your longing be hijacked by common sense for fear of being swept away.

Allow yourself to be swept away by the heart's wisdom!

2

If you already know that the purpose of human life is to wake up, recognize this as great good fortune.

Organize your life around finding out what's actually here. Don't listen to fear-based advice!

You have already tasted naturalness and goodness. Remain seated at the banquet of the wisdom heart.

Consistent spiritual practice will relieve you of your strongest attachments.

Don't struggle to renounce. You will relinquish attachments when the time is ripe. Or they will be taken. Just don't resist when you notice your cherished ones walking out the door.

Whatever remains will help you to wake up.

4

God is always responding.

Look for the wisdom in every circumstance. Keep looking. Follow wisdom! She never lets go of your hand. Don't give yourself an out by listening to ordinary mind!

Out, in this case, will just add years to your sentence in the prison of limitation.

5

Everything is fine! Whatever happens is beneficial.

You say God is All and One. Then you complain that things are going wrong. Who is your God anyway?

Keep on complaining if you like, but laugh at yourself, or at least raise an eyebrow.

6

If you are making up spiritual explanations and experiences, recognize that you lack confidence.

Have mercy on yourself. Confidence only grows by finding out what is really being offered here.

Drop all attitudes, explanations, goals, exaggerations and stories. Just practice. Let Reality lead you. You won't be disappointed.

Caring one iota about winning, acclaim, measuring up or having a lot of students just means your rank is beginner.

Examine your motivations and intentions with the eye of Jupiter. Be as sober and uncompromising with yourself as Lord Saturn.

Take off your shoes. Sit down.

8

Hardly anyone knows how to be a disciple, yet so many are teachers.

This Reality is in a state of continual worship, offering itself into itself. You can't join the party if you hold anything back.

Eventually you will have to graduate from being a teacher to being a devotee.

9

So now you want to be a great disciple? You are already lost.

The Lord plays so many tricks. You think you are out of the fun house, but it's just another mirror with your same old scary face grinning back.

There is nothing to do but give up and be honest.

10

Everyone arrives here in a different condition. You have no other treasure.

If you aren't willing to begin walking from where you are, you will eventually have to backtrack and start over. This is a cosmic law.

So don't even bother with self-aggrandizement, imitation and lies.

"Stop struggling; stop meddling" is the best meditation advice. No more attacking Reality with plans, pronouncements, fantasies and projections. No more fixing and fiddling. No more witnessing, narrating or making anything out of it all.

You'd think it would be easy to relax and drop all that effort. Ha!

Just sitting is not for the lazy.

12

Live life as if you are playing a game. The game involves continually rounding a corner and responding spontaneously and cheerfully to whatever you encounter.

Leave your body, mind and energy fresh and uncontrived.

Sure, make plans, but don't expect anything to come of them.

To whom are you bragging? Who are you trying to convince? Whose opinion are you manipulating? Who are you defending? Who are you criticizing? Whose criticism are you warding off?

God, only you, you, you.

14

Earnestness, brow-beating, self-depreciation and doggedness won't work. They're just tricks little self uses to stay alive while trying to look like it's on the way out.

Stop all that frantic arm waving. Quiet down.

Let wisdom take care of the character assassination.

15

If you can't yet integrate with presence in every moment, meditate. If you can't meditate, chant. If you can't chant, do puja. If you can't do puja, sing. If you can't sing, read teachings. If you can't read teachings, do some service. Look at pictures of your teacher. Hang out with spiritual friends. Breathe Hamsa, or Om Ma. Always come to satsang.

You are in a leaky boat. But you have innumerable ways to plug up the holes and cracks.

God is the boat, the holes and the plugs. Whee!

16

Fashion yourself a habitable life. A job. A place to live. Some friends. Maybe a love. Kids if you like.

A person on the road to waking up benefits from alliances and support. Satisfy yourself.

Just don't make a big deal about it. Don't let yourself get eaten by life.

17

Everything you have will be taken from you, and in short order, too.

There is nothing of this world you can keep, other than your awakeness.

Try to remember that, even as you tend lovingly to life.

18

This body will die soon, but it can help you to discover what never dies.

Don't worry about aging. Make a continual effort to reintegrate with your real nature, and you will become fearless. Only that livingness is immortal.

There is both poignancy and majesty in this life.

What do you really want? The answer is right there, in your heart of hearts.

Why shouldn't you have it? You should!

Next time around, you could show up as a banana slug. What will you be capable of wanting then?

20

Your clock is on methamphetamine. Patience is a great freedom.

Recalibrate, child of eternity!

A ttachment to spiritual accomplishment is an obstacle. The point is to become unconditioned.

And anyway, you will never arrive. Where God, the Self, is concerned, there is only a play of arriving.

Don't cling to anything but aware livingness.

22

You can't know the results of your spiritual practices in advance. And anyway, whatever you imagine is conditioned.

The only way to find out is to practice, day by day, through every circumstance.

In the face of that, the Mother cannot help but reveal herself.

Eka rasa, one taste, does not mean no likes or dislikes. It means seeing the real nature of whatever appears, even your own attachments.

Living like this instantly liberates and brings laughter, patience and compassion.

24

There is no View, no mission and no path. Liberation changes nothing. Reality is already perfected, wide awake from the start.

My Guru taught that spiritual practice is nothing but playfulness. Get in the game! Find out!

You are the beloved child of *that*.

ABOUT JAYA KULA

Jaya Kula is a 501(c)3 nonprofit spiritual community with centers in Portland, Maine and Portland, Oregon. We offer opportunities to learn and practice in the traditions of direct realization Tantra (Trika Shaivism) and Anandamayi Ma. Shambhavi Sarasvati is our spiritual director.

Jaya Kula Press is owned by Shambhavi Sarasvati.

Mailing address:

110 Marginal Way, #196

Portland, ME 04101

Email: sayhi@jayakula.org

Phone: 207.358.0121

Visit jayakula.org for more information about our offerings.

Jaya Kula Press Titles by Shambhavi Sarasvati

Pilgrims to Openness: Direct Realization Tantra in Everyday Life, 2009

Tantra: the Play of Awakening, 2012

Returning: Exhortations, Advice and Encouragement from the Heart of Direct Realization Practice, 2015

Reality Sutras: the View of Direct Realization Tantra, forthcoming 2016